fine cigarettes

Kensitas
famous gifts

Harry Fenton

Smart
Weston

CIGARETTES
FINLAYS
CONFECTIONERY

LEWIS'S
Jewellers

HARTS

Remember Sheffield
in the 50s, 60s and 70s

by David Richardson

Printed & Published by Pickard Publishing,

10-11 Riverside Park, Sheaf Gardens, Sheffield S2 4BB

Telephone 0114 275 7222 or 275 7444

Facsimile 0114 275 8866

Remember Sheffield
in the 50s, 60s, and 70s

My earliest recollections are perhaps those of the winter of '47, 1947 if anyone wonders. The house where we lived enjoyed an elevated position, being at the top of some twenty steps. Heavy drifting snow seemed to bring us down to the same level as the rest of Pitsmoor. The windows iced up both inside and out, but these were days long before central heating, double-glazing and global warming.

In the summer, the allotment garden provided us with vegetables that were otherwise unavailable. At the allotment society hut, old men smoked pipes of revolting tobacco that they had grown and cured themselves. They bought pea and bean seeds by the gill which were measured in an old tankard. At least they weren't paying for expensive packaging, and sheer volume assured good germination. Colorado Beetle and Dig for Victory posters abounded and it seemed that the members were still at war. Stories of the war were told with great enthusiasm and I thought that most people actually enjoyed it. There was the bomb that fell just outside our shelter, making a 20 foot hole but which failed to explode, fire watching in the A.R.P., rationing and the black market. All very exciting!

Then there were the trips to town. Sheffielders had to go to town every week and I couldn't understand why it was called town and not city. We always went on the tram, since not many families owned motor cars in those days. The evidence of the war was very clear: big craters, burnt out buildings and the re-building. At first they built single storey premises where large shops had been. Later more concrete was added to start the new trend of characterless buildings. In the '50s, re-development began. The City Council and the Developers took over where Hitler had left off and, at first by stealth, lovely old buildings were replaced by concrete monstrosities. Public protests and campaigns made no difference, and we are lucky that we have any buildings of merit left. For instance, that we have the Lyceum Theatre to admire and enjoy is indeed a miracle. We are, however, more fortunate than many large cities in the number of historic buildings remaining, and amongst other campaigners, the work of the Hallamshire Historic Buildings Society must be recognised.

The other great mistake was the final abandonment of the trams in 1960. We had, perhaps the finest tramway system in the country, but again the City Fathers knew best. They said the trams were inflexible, expensive and unable to flow with other traffic. The 'Star' ran a campaign 'The City's Thrombosis', claiming that the trams were clogging up the traffic in the streets. With car ownership increasing exponentially at the time, it is hardly surprising that this was the popular view. No one even thought about the future when the streets would be blocked solid with cars and we would have to reconsider the superiority of the tram for carrying a large number of people in comfort and at speed.

This book is designed to bring back memories of the Sheffield we knew in the '50s, 60s and '70s: lest we forget. One thing we do tend to forget is just how black the buildings were at the time, since we tend to glamorize the past. The Clean Air Act did not come into being until 1956, and it was enforced area by area over a number of years. You will, however, notice a distinct lack of litter in the streets. Perhaps we are more careless now and maybe modern packaging contributes to the problem. Despite all my complaints about the mistakes of the past, we still have a great city to live in, and it is getting better. One thing that I would strongly recommend is that everyone with a camera should record the changing scene for posterity.

Remember: today's photograph is tomorrow's historical record.

Many of the photographs in this book are from my own collection, but others are borrowed from friends, and some are from the archive of the Sheffield Libraries, Archives and Information, Local Studies Department. I am particularly grateful to Howard Turner and Jack Wrigley for their unstinting help and advice and for access to their extensive collections of photographs of the area. Credit is due to them for their wisdom and foresight in photographing our city at perhaps its time of greatest change. I am also indebted to the following people for help and encouragement in preparing this collection of photographs of the city centre: Ray Heard, Mick Liversidge, Ray Myers, Mike Spick and the late J. Edward Vickers M.B.E. In particular, I must thank my wife, Margaret, who has endured the large amount of clutter that the compilation of this book has created and has examined the text for grammatical errors. Without the help of these people, this book would have remained a dream project for sometime in the future.

David Richardson
Sheffield 2002

Remember Sheffield

Part 1

The '50s

High Street, 1950

On a sunny shopping day, the people of Sheffield get back to enjoying themselves again after a prolonged period of severe restraint enforced by World War 11. Note the burnt out Walsh's building on the right, Burton's on the left and the crater where Marples once stood.

Photograph Press Agency, courtesy Sheffield Libraries, Archives and Information, Local Studies

High Street, March 1954

This photograph of the bombed Burton Building at the corner of High Street and Angel Street typifies the austerity of the era. Grey, bombed out buildings, heavy overcoats and hats, and little in the way of commercial cheer. There was, however, always a tram in sight and these splendid vehicles ran to most parts of the city and would get you home in comfort.
Photograph J.H. Turner

Moorhead, 1958.

Quite a sprinkling of private cars by now. Jays, the furniture shop, was very enterprising, sporting the largest facia in Sheffield at the time.
Photograph J.H.Turner

The Moor, January 1950

This view of the Moor and Button Lane is typical of Sheffield in the '50s. There is a theory that enemy aircraft mistook the Moor for the industrial East End. Certainly there was plenty of bomb damage.

Photograph Press Photo Agency, courtesy Sheffield Libraries, Archives and Information, Local Studies

The Moor, September 1950

Atkinson's had received a direct hit in the blitz, but they bravely put on a window display at the devastated site. Meanwhile, they moved to temporary premises and continued trading. Interestingly, they are still at the original site today.

Photograph Press Photo Agency, courtesy Sheffield Libraries, Archives and Information, Local Studies

Fargate from East Parade, 1958
The City centre returning to normality after a long period of austerity. All the buildings in Fargate are intact, and the Cathedral gates have escaped the fate of much of the iron work in the City which was melted down to help the war effort.
Photograph J.A. Walton

Market Place, April 1958
Another example of the start of the consumer spending era, this time in the pouring rain.
Photograph J.R. Wrigley

Commercial Street, May 1957
Little, if anything, remains of the buildings in this photograph. Only the lie of the land gives this location away to those who don't remember Sheffield in the '50s.
Photograph J.R. Wrigley

Path from Arundel Lane to Pond Street, March 1957
This scene is probably even less recognisable. The Anderson Shelter panels, used here for fencing, remind us just how difficult it was to get materials.
Photograph J.R. Wrigley

Sheaf Street, June 1958
Sheaf Street was always a busy spot even before the giant roundabout arrived.
Photograph J.A. Walton

Sheaf Street, June 1958
In this shot, we have the Corn Exchange on the left and Castlefolds Market on the right.
Photograph J.A. Walton

Sheaf Market, March 1959.
If only we could walk, once again, through the old "Rag & Tag Market" and gaze in amazement at the stalls which included such wonders as Joe (Potty) Edwards, Aaron Patnick ("Come on all you bookworms"), Joe Fellowes (market gardener) and N.R. Bardwell (surplus electronics). Looming in the background is a large building project - Park Hill flats.
Photograph C.J. Farrant

Dixon Lane from Sheaf Market, March 1959
The scene from the entrance to the Sheaf Market shows just how popular this area was. The large building in the centre of the picture is the rear of the, soon to be demolished, Norfolk Market Hall, while the rickety building on the right is the Castlefolds wholesale fruit and vegetable market.
Photograph C.J. Farrant

Commercial Street, Sheaf Street Junction, September 1959
Here we have the back entrance to the Sheaf Market, and a leisurely scene. This corner now forms a part of what is probably the busiest roundabout in Sheffield.
Photograph C.J. Farrant

Shude Hill, May 1959
Another intriguing view of the Sheaf Market, this time framed by the Commercial Street road bridge.
Photograph C.J. Farrant

Broad Street, 1957

An atmospheric photograph of the Castlefolds wholesale fruit and vegetable market with the Corn Exchange in the background.

Photograph Sheffield Libraries, Archives and Information, Local Studies

Broad Street, 1959

Another photograph of the Castlefolds Market. Maybe we should reconsider horse drawn carts to cut down on pollution.

Photograph Sheffield Libraries, Archives and Information, Local Studies

Sheaf Street from Granville Street ramp, May 1959
How many will remember this short cut from the Park district to the town? Before us lie Commercial Street, the Sheaf Market, and the Corn Exchange.
Photograph C.J. Farrant

Gilbert Street from Sheaf Street ramp, May 1959
Another view from the Sheaf Street ramp, this time over the railway line to the Sun Inn and Park Hill flats which were just being built. These units were designed to be the future, the answer to slum clearance.
Photograph C.J. Farrant

Norfolk Market Hall, 1958

Two views of the Norfolk Market Hall, one from Castle Street and the other from King Street. What a shame it was demolished! An old fashioned market hall would now have been a great attraction.

Photographs J.A. Walton

Norfolk Market Hall interior, 1959

This lovely interior photograph reminds us of its wide diversity of traders.

Photograph Market Superintendent, courtesy Sheffield Libraries, Archives and Information, Local Studies

Exchange Street, June 1957
An early morning (7.45 a.m.) view of Exchange Street and side elevation of the Norfolk Market Hall. Note the utilitarian tram shelter, Thomas Furniss for pets and pet food and John Mace Ltd., Corn Merchants.
Photograph J.A. Walton

Dixon Lane, April 1959
Another rare view of the side of the Norfolk Market Hall, this time from Dixon Lane. It looks like another early morning shot. Posed on the steps is the photographer's daughter.
Photograph J.A. Walton

Pond Street, April 1958

The building site in the foreground is for the new technical college which was later to become Hallam University. The complex of single storey buildings on the corner of Harmer Lane was a "British Restaurant" which was set up by the government as an emergency war-time measure. The Corporation later took over the running of all the "British Restaurants" in the City and re-named them "Civic Restaurants". They closed down in the late '50s.

Photograph J.R. Wrigley

Flat Street, October 1959

A busy Saturday with shoppers streaming down Flat Street to the buses in Pond Street. Nobody appears to be concerned that this is the last day of trams on the Wadsley Bridge to Woodseats route.

Photograph J.A Walton

High Street, June 1952
Policemen on point duty controlled the traffic which consisted mainly of trams and pedestrians.
Photograph City Engineers Department, courtesy Sheffield Libraries, Archives and Information, Local Studies

High Street, May 1959
We still had policemen on point duty and central reservations where we could catch a tram to various parts of the City.
Photograph C.J. Farrant

Chapel Walk, June 1959
It's hard to believe that Chapel Walk was as narrow as this at the Norfolk Street end, at the time when the thoroughfare was less commercial than it is now.
Photograph J.A.Walton

Chapel Walk, June 1959
The Fargate end had plenty of specialist shops which have now disappeared or moved to the shopping mall or been incorporated into the supermarkets.
Photograph J.A. Walton

Fargate, December 1957
Shoppers and private motorcars were out in force, and to add to the joy there was a giant Christmas tree.
Photograph J.R. Wrigley

High Street, January 1958
Shoppers out again, this time to snap up bargains in the January sales.
Photograph J. R. Wrigley

Town Hall and Peace Gardens October 1957

The area at the side of the Town Hall was officially named St. Paul's Gardens after the church which fronted on to Pinstone Street. It soon became known as the Peace Gardens, possibly because of its association with the postponement of the second world war and Neville Chamberlain's announcement of "Peace in our time"

Photograph C.J. Farrant

Peace Gardens and Norfolk Street, September 1959

For whatever reason the Peace Gardens got its name, it soon became popular as a place to sit in peace and tranquillity, during fine weather of course.

Photograph J.A. Walton

Moorhead, September 1957

Moorhead, intact in 1957, spared by Hitler's bombs, but soon to be demolished to make way for more concrete. The car parked in the temporary car park on the right appears to have overstayed its welcome.

Photograph J.A. Walton

Button Lane and Pinstone Street from the Moor, September 1957

A good example of the use of single storey temporary shops is shown by the Freeman, Hardy and Willis shoe shop. Note that the billboard is almost as big as the shop itself.

Photograph J.A. Walton

The Moor, November 1952

The left hand side of the Moor, heading out of town had all the businesses we needed: Weaver to Wearer for suits; a public house (the Pump Tavern); further down Cussins for furniture; Shapero for floor covering and Blaskeys for decorating materials.

Photograph Press Photo Agency, courtesy Sheffield Libraries, Archives and Information, Local Studies

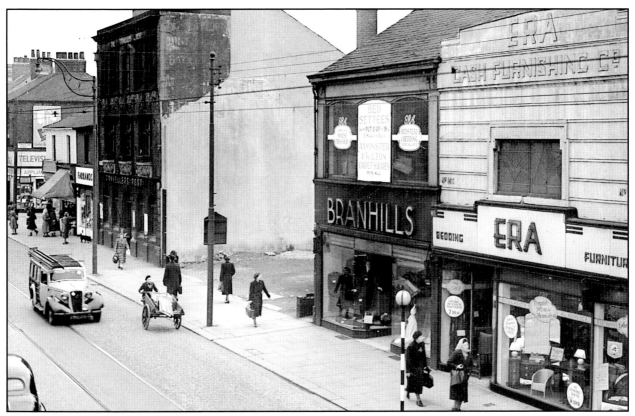

The Moor, November 1952

Lower down the Moor, after Cumberland Street, we had a tobacconist, fruiterer, grocer and public house (Travellers' Rest). Next came Branhills, costumier and Era furnishing. What else could we want? - Money perhaps.

Photograph Press Photo Agency, courtesy Sheffield Libraries, Archives and Information, Local Studies

Moorfoot, November 1950
Moorfoot, early '50s. Note the small traffic island and ancient vehicles.
Photograph Sheffield Libraries, Archives and Information, Local Studies

Moorfoot, April 1959
Less than ten years later and there is a large roundabout and more evidence of modern, privately owned vehicles.
Photograph C.J. Farrant

Part 2

The
Transport Scene

High Street, July 1958
On a wet day in summer, car 63 makes its way through the city streets.
Photograph J.A. Walton

Fitzalan Square, 1955.

Car No 479 , built in Sheffield by Cravens in 1927, makes its way through Fitzalan Square.
Photograph J.H. Turner

Conquering Hero, Atlantean Bus, Flat Street, 1959.

The Atlantean seen here, close to an example of the tram it was to replace, marked a major development in bus design at the time. It had all-inclusive bodywork, folding doors operated by the driver, heaters and the ability to go anywhere. However, they were subject to quite a few mechanical problems, note the oil spill down the side. They were not very comfortable, and would prove to be quite slow, especially since they were soon to be held up by a growing number of private motorcars. Looking back, it would seem that their only advantage was the cream and blue livery.
Photograph J.H. Turner

High Street, Haymarket, March 1957

Sometimes the operation of a tramway system requires specialised repairs to its infrastructure. Here we see track renewal which involves removal of the stone setts and tar boiling equipment for their replacement. Two lads look on fascinated with the work.

Photograph T. I. Robinson

Pinstone Street, April 1957

Another occurance specific to tramways. As a tram had lost its trolleyhead, emergency repairs by the overhead gang in the AEC tower wagon were necessary.

Photograph B. Mettam

Angel Street, October 2nd 1960

On the Sunday before the closure of the Sheffield tramway system, a group of enthusiasts hired special trams to take them round the remaining track. They knew what a loss the city was suffering, but it looked as if no one else cared.
Photograph C.P.H. Robinson

Pinstone Street, 8th October 1960

Less than one week later on a very wet Saturday night, it seemed as if the entire population had turned out to say goodbye to the trams that had served them so well.
Photograph D.J. Richardson

Moorhead, October 8th 1960
The last day of the trams in Sheffield. This photograph is symbolic of the situation: trams finishing, Crimean Monument reduced to its base, and a big skip on the left hand side, to take away the old rubbish!
Photograph J.R.Wrigley

High Street, October 15th 1960
Just one week after the closure of the tram system, evidence of their existence is being removed with indecent haste. Note that only span wires and attachments remain of the overhead, and the points have been filled in with asphalt.
Photograph J.R. Wrigley

The Moor, December 1961

Just over one year after the closure of the tramway system in Sheffield, a tram returned to the streets. Horse tram 15 was borrowed from the Crich Tramway Museum to run on the rails which were still in evidence on The Moor.

Photograph D.J. Richardson

High Street, December 1961

Horse tram 15 was put on display as part of the Christmas celebrations for 1961, just to show that we were already missing the trams. On this Sunday morning in December, the snow and the Salvation Army band, added to the poignancy of the scene.

Photograph J.H. Turner

Midland Station, October 1959
The bus, a Leyland PD2, had already served the city well for eleven years when this photograph was taken. But note its cared for appearance, afforded by the high standard of maintenance from the Sheffield Corporation Transport Department. Behind the bus is a 1938 Lagonda, quite a rare vehicle even in 1959.
Photograph T.I. Robinson

Fitzalan Square, April 1966
A 1947 built Leyland PD2 still going strong after 19 years of service. This one was from the first batch supplied with Leyland bodywork after the war. The bus is on a workman's service run, route 119, from Vulcan Road to Scarsdale Road.
Photograph J.H. Turner

Pond Hill, May 1966

Leyland Titan PD2 with C.H. Roe bodywork, No. 834, one of 95 Leylands supplied during 1957-58. Since this time, Pond Hill has changed beyond recognition, but here we see the stark contrast between the concrete and glass building used by the Post Office and the old Victorian factory facing Flat Street, the old gas lamp and the long gone Lyceum Hotel with its glazed tiling exterior.

Photograph J.H. Turner

Glossop Road/Gell Street, June 1972

One of the handsome Roe bodied Leyland PD3 double deckers entering Glossop Road on the long route from Crookes to Woodhouse. One of these vehicles, No 904 survives painted in full Sheffield Corporation colours of cream and blue and can often be seen on private hire work.

Photograph J.H. Turner

Church Street, September 1973

In the last year of Sheffield Corporation Transport, a park Royal A.E.C. Regent V waits to depart for Nether Edge Hospital with three rear engined buses in the background.

Photograph J.H. Turner

Sheaf Street, June 1977

On this Saturday in June, traffic had been diverted from the city centre due to the Lord Mayor's Parade. This vantage point became a bus enthusiasts' paradise and we can see examples of vehicles in the old S.T.D. as well as the new S.Y.P.T.E. liveries.

Photograph J.H. Turner

High Street, September 1975

In this photograph we see a brand new Leyland National, number 84, on the City Clipper route. On the other side of High Street is a Leyland Atlantean still in its Sheffield Corporation cream and blue livery.

Photograph J.H. Turner

Pinstone Street, June 1979

A German M.A.N. Bendibus, one of the first batch of five to operate in Sheffield, on the City Clipper route seen from the upper floor of Thomas Cook's Travel Agency, during the Lord Mayor's Parade.

Photograph J.H. Turner

Bridge Street Bus Station, March 1974

The policy of restricting the number of buses which passed through the town centre, resulted in Bridge Street Bus Station as terminus for routes to the north side of the city. Not so good for the passengers who had to climb Snig Hill and Angel Street to get to the shops.

Photograph J.R. Wrigley

Holly Street, November 1973

No such difficulty for the private motorist, however, who could still take his car to most parts of the central area and leave it conveniently near to the big stores.

Photograph J.R. Wrigley

Midland Station, September 1965

The cleaned-up facade of the Midland Station, plus water feature with Park Hill Flats as a backdrop.
Photograph J .A. Walton

Victoria Station and Royal Victoria Hotel from Furnival Road, August 1965

A rare and unusual shot from the top of a buttress to a wall on Furnival Road. The rail service to Manchester was withdrawn early in 1970, and this resulted in the closure of Victoria Station.
Photograph J.R. Wrigley

Midland Station, May 1958

The driver of LMS Jubilee class 4.6.0, No. 45598 is inspecting his engine. LMS Compound 4.4.0 No. 41119 is stabled in the bay platform 7, while B.R. Standard class 5.4.6.0 waits to pull out bound for Bristol Temple Meads. The terraced houses in the background were on Granville Street which now forms part of the Supertram route to Halfway.
Photograph J.H. Turner

Victoria Station, June 1959

Great Central Improved Director class 4.4.0 No. 62661 'Gerard Powys Dewhurst' is the 5.49 p.m. slow train to Leicester Central. LNER B1 class 4.6.0 No. 61406 is waiting to take over from an electric engine on a Manchester to Cleethorpes express, whilst a Cravens of Darnall built diesel railcar is on the local service to Doncaster.
Photograph J.H. Turner

View from Pitsmoor Road, July 1963

Once we had a fast electric rail link with Manchester. Will it ever be reinstated?

Photograph J.R. Wrigley

Victoria Station, May 1964

This train has just arrived from Manchester. Note the unusual circular windscreen wipers. A few years later when it had been decided that we no longer needed a fast electric rail line to Manchester, this engine and others were sold to the Dutch Railways for further service.

Photograph J.H. Turner

Canal Wharf, 1969

The Tinsley to Sheffield section of the canal opened in 1819, but the coming of the railways really brought a gradual decline of heavy goods carriage by this means. This photograph was taken one year before the last of the commercial users ceased carrying goods on the canal.

Photograph J.H. Turner

Canal Basin, April 1965

This fine photograph shows an often forgotten side of the city centre. In the distance is the tower of the Electric Supply Offices. The Spider T was bringing grain for Aizlewood's flour mill. She was built in 1925 as a sloop with two sails and an engine by Warren of New Holland for J.J.Tomlinson of Thorne.

Photograph J .R. Wrigley

Part 3
The '60s

Lyceum Theatre, 1966
The '60s was a decade of great change for Sheffield as illustrated by this photograph. In this scene, the Lyceum is dark in theatrical terms, but at least it is still being used. All around there is evidence of re-development.
Photograph J.R. Wrigley

Shude Lane, August 1965
Few will remember the back streets where the Ponds Forge Complex now stands.
Photograph J.R. Wrigley

Sheaf Lane, August 1965
Even fewer will be able to name this location without reading the caption. Sheaf Lane was off the bottom of Broad Street, across from Dixon Lane and was often used by market traders for storing their wares. This area disappeared under the Park Square roundabout many years ago.
Photograph J.R. Wrigley

Corn Exchange, Sheaf Street, June 1962

In keeping with his role of major landowner in the area, the Duke of Norfolk had the Corn Exchange built in 1881. Despite the fact that it had been seriously damaged by fire in 1947, the facade appeared to be in good condition. Certainly, offices were still operating in the building up to this time.

Photograph J.A. Walton.

Corn Exchange demolition, May 1963

Too late. Another fine building bites the dust.

Photograph J.A. Walton.

Granville Street steps, September 1960
Great contrasts in this photograph. Steps worn with constant use, old premises, new flats and modern motorcars.
All now long gone.
Photograph C.J. Farrant

Wicker, August 1964

LMS 'Jubilee' 4.6.0 No 45581, 'Bihar and Orissa' on Wicker Bridge working a return holiday train from Poole to Bradford. Wicker Viaduct was completed in December 1848. Note the old Wicker Goods Depot beyond the bridge. The site was the first station in Sheffield, built by the Sheffield and Rotherham Railway and opened in 1838.

Photograph J.H. Turner

Lady's Bridge, April 1963

The other famous bridge in Sheffield. This photograph shows clearly how the bridge has been widened and extra supports added. It also shows the extent of Tennants brewery.

Photograph J.H. Turner

Haymarket, June 1961

On this page can be seen the old and the new. The Woolworth building had served the City well for many years and here it is as popular as ever.

Photograph C.J. Farrant

Exchange Street, June 1961

Just a few yards around the corner, the incomplete Castle Market is already showing signs of popularity.

Photograph C.J. Farrant

Sheaf Market, August 1965

We tend to remember the past with a fondness that makes things seem better than they were. Certainly, by 1965, the Sheaf Market was worthy of its nick name, 'Rag and Tag'.

Photograph J.R. Wrigley

Sheaf Market, August 1965

Another corner of the 'Rag and Tag'. Note the neat method of waste disposal.

Photograph J.R. Wrigley

Angel Street, May 1960
Single tram track, overhead wiring, a line-up of classic cars and the Leyland bus in S.T.D. livery indicate the very early '60s.
Photograph C.J. Farrant

Angel Street, May 1960
The entrance to the Black Swan, popularly known as the "Mucky Duck". This pub was soon to become the venue for some of the best known local and internationally famous rock'n roll groups and turns.
Photograph C.J. Farrant

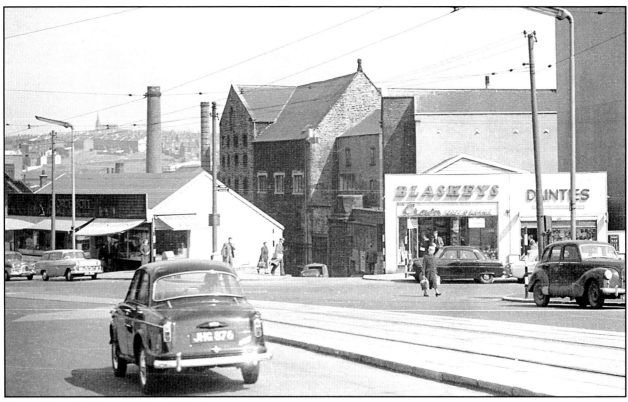

From Angel Street, May 1960
Snig Hill to the left, Castle Street to the right, and Water Lane descending in the middle.
Photograph C.J. Farrant

Water Lane, August 1965
Not many readers will be willing to admit that they recognise this corner of Sheffield: the Police Charge Office. Note the lads from a Z Cars episode about to enter the Nick.
Photograph J.R. Wrigley

Two of Sheffield's oldest watering holes are the Mulberrry Tavern (left) and the Old Queen's Head (below). The Mulberry Tavern is said to have been on this site since the early 1800's and there has been a building on the site of the Old Queen's Head for at least 400 years. The public house part of the building was, however, the building on the left for many years until it was extended into the ancient part which is recognised as the Old Queen's Head today.

Mulberry Tavern, Mulberry Street, April 1964   *Photograph J.A. Walton*

Old Queen's Head, Pond Hill, March 1964   *Photograph D.J. Richardson*

Angel Street, 1960
In this view of Angel Street there are examples of temporary shops after blitz damage.   The Co-op has erected a single storey building, whilst the branch of Syminton and Croft, the fancy drapers, is using its ground floor to continue trading.
Photograph C.J. Farrant

Castle Street and Angel Street, April 1964
By 1964 the B & C Co-op had got its new store ready for opening.
Photograph C.J. Farrant

Cathedral, May 1964
Work on the extension to the Cathedral had begun.
Photograph C.J. Farrant

Cathedral, June 1965
Just over one year later and we were able to enjoy the new building.
Photograph C.J. Farrant

Sheffield from Bungay Street, August 1965
This fine view covers the Midland Railway Station, the Dyson Refractories building, Howard Hotel, Howard Street and the new Technical College.
Photograph J.R. Wrigley

Sheffield from Bungay Street, August 1965
What a panorama! In the foreground, Granville Street, the Midland Station and Pond Street bus station. The skyline includes the Town Hall, St. Marie's, Victoria Hall, Cathedral and Kemsley House.
Photograph J.R. Wrigley

Sycamore Street, Tudor Way, May 1960
If you can't remember what things were like B.C. (before the Crucible), this is it. At the bottom of Sycamore Street, in the middle of the picture, is part of the G.P.O. complex on Flat Street.
Photograph C.J. Farrant

Arundel Street, May 1960
The scene from the steps of the Lyceum with Norfolk Street to the left of the picture.
Photograph C.J. Farrant

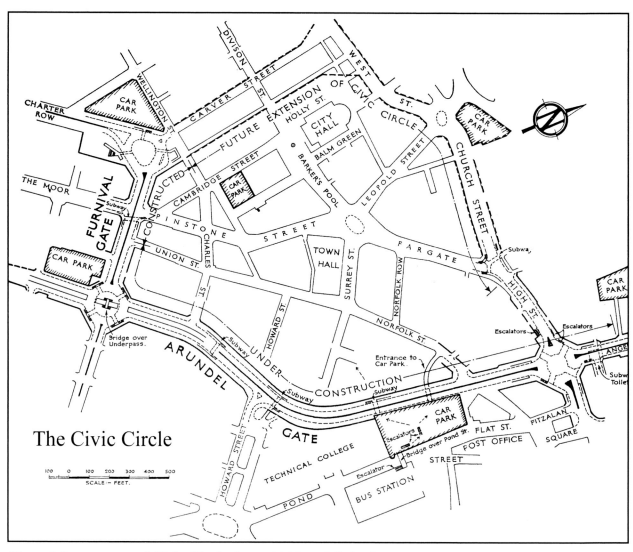

The Civic Circle

Map of the proposed Civic Circle from 1967 publicity leaflet

Do you remember all the publicity about the Civic Circle? It certainly was a grand scale project and, by the time this map was published, the first section (Furnival Gate) had already been completed. Sadly this work had caused the destruction of quite a few fine buildings at Moorhead, such as the Newton Chamber's city offices. The next stage marked "under construction" in this map was quite a feat of civil engineering with the underpass at the Furnival Gate, Arundel Gate roundabout and the large project at High Street, which would soon become known as the "Hole in the Road". The idea seemed to be that pedestrians should go underground and vehicular traffic would reign supreme on the surface. Fortunately, the remainder of the Civic Circle project was never completed. Looking at it now, it would seem that the planners were more foresighted than we realised. Arundel Gate would make an ideal alignment for an extension of the Supertram to take its much needed services to the south western suburbs of the city.

The new Arundel Gate takes shape, September 1965

Photographs C.J. Farrant

Photograph C.J. Farrant

Photograph C.J. Farrant

Photograph M. Liversidge

High Street, 1966
Sheffield was about to get a new feature, the Castle Roundabout, or "Hole in the Road" as it became known. These photographs give some idea of the disruption which its building caused.

Change Alley, May 1960

One of the long-lost streets of Sheffield is Change Alley. It ran between High Street and Norfolk Street, and it was demolished in 1964 to form part of the alignment of Arundel Gate.

Photograph C.J. Farrant

Fitzalan Square, April 1964

Whatever happened to the Fitzalan Square we knew? Barclay's Bank was damaged by fire, the Classic Cinema closed, the Bell Hotel and Sleep Shop made way for more modern retail units and, of course, Wigfall's is no more. You may remember that 'Wiggies' is where many Sheffielders got their electrical appliances, especially t.v. sets which, in those days, were expensive and unreliable.

Photograph C.J. Farrant

Norfolk Street and Fitzalan Square, April 1964

Next to nothing now remains of this corner of Sheffield. The Elephant Inn and the buildings at the bottom side of Fitzalan Square are all long gone. Perhaps the area did need a bit of tidying, but complete extermination was not necessary.

Photograph C.J. Farrant

Corner of Fargate and Church Street, April 1963

Cole's Corner was such a popular meeting place that it was hard to believe that the building had become too small for the John Lewis Partnership and was about to close. However, the crane in the distance at the left hand side of the picture was already working on the new department store. It was many years before we stopped saying "See you at Cole' s Corner".
Photograph C.J. Farrant

Barker's Pool, April 1964

Just one year later, and Cole Brothers are in their new department store.
Photograph C.J. Farrant

Goodwin Fountain, Fargate, May 1964
This site had been a rockery for many years, but in 1961, Sir Stuart and Lady Goodwin presented a large water feature to the City.
Photograph C.J. Farrant

Barker's Pool, September 1960
Not far away, in Barker's Pool, was the stainless steel globe.
Photograph J.A. Walton

View from Pond Street, September 1960

Quite a large project on awkward terrain, but a least there are a few fine old buildings still standing.

Photograph C.J. Farrant

View from Howard Street, August 1965

Five years later, and still there is a lot to be done on the re-construction front, but what happened to the old buildings? That's progress. Note the motor vehicle tax office in its temporary accommodation to the left of the picture.

Photograph J.R. Wrigley

Norfolk Lane and Tudor Street, September 1960

All these buildings were demolished to make way for the Town Hall extension. Through the archway, we can see the site of the Crucible Theatre.

Photograph J.A. Walton

Tudor Street from Surrey Street, April 1964

The corner of the Central Library on the extreme right of this photograph and the tower of the Victoria Hall are the only remaining reference points. All the other buildings have gone to make way for the plaza in front of the Crucible and Lyceum Theatres.

Photograph C.J. Farrant

Surrey Street, April 1964

From left to right, the Central Library, Surrey Street Methodist Church and the Army Recruiting Centre. This fine building was originally the Sheffield Medical School. The only bit of this building still in existence is the motto: "Ars longa, vita brevis" which is now outside the Royal Hallamshire Hospital. Don't we know this to be true!

Photograph C.J. Farrant

Norfolk Street April 1964.

Was it a Sunday morning, or perhaps a flag day? In the centre of the photograph is the opening to a thoroughfare which no longer exists - Cadman Lane. All these properties were demolished for the Town Hall extension in 1973 which later became known as the Egg Box. The square tower at the right hand side marks the position of Walker & Hall's showroom.
Photograph C.J. Farrant

Norfolk Street April 1964.

A view of the lower end of Norfolk Street showing an early Thornton's Chocolate Kabin at the end of Change Alley. On the other corner is Thomas Ashton, Engineers and Engineers' Furnishers. It is now hard to believe that such a business could exist in the city centre.
Photograph C.J. Farrant

So you think you knew Sheffield in the 1960s?

No 1 *Photograph C.J. Farrant*

No 2 *Photograph C.J. Farrant*

No 3 *Photograph J.R. Wrigley*

No 4 *Photograph J.A. Walton*

1 Arundel Street, showing the back of Surrey Street
   Methodist Chapel.

2 Norfolk Street showing the Sheffield Club which was a
   gentlemens' club.

3 Sycamore Street, looking down towards Flat Street.

4 Backfields, which connected the Moor with West Street.

Orchard Street from Leopold Street, April 1961
In this picture, the Assay Office on the left already has a death sentence hanging over it in the form of a demolition notice from James Childs. This company had the dubious privilege of demolishing many of Sheffield's most interesting buildings.
Photograph J.A. Walton

Pinstone Street, May 1964

The top end of Cambridge Arcade. What memories! Barney Goodman, Sugg's, Sheffield United Tours and the blind man who sold packets of lavender and matches.

Photograph D.J. Richardson

Union Street, October 1969

The bottom end of Cambridge Arcade, and one of the few cafes in Sheffield at the time.

Photograph C.J. Farrant

Cambridge Arcade, June 1961

Not the same grandeur as the arcades in Leeds, but Cambridge Arcade could have been a great feature of the City had it been retained. Photographers will remember that Hodgson's camera shop was on the left.
Photograph C.J. Farrant

The Moor, July 1960
Here, Roberts Brothers were already trading in their new department store, but were still using other units nearby, such as the one to the left of this picture, together with their original premises which can be seen in the distance to the right.
Photograph J.A. Walton

The Moor, September 1960
Lower down The Moor, the Sheffield and Ecclesall Co-op had moved into their new premises. The re-establishment of The Moor as a major trading area was an important stage in the recovery of Sheffield after the war.
Photograph J.A. Walton

Button Lane from Moorhead, July 1960.

These premises, built in the 1820s, were soon to be demolished to make way for Charter Square. Note the wall mounted gas lamp, the Angel Inn with its side entrance and the shops that Roberts Brothers had been using until their new department store opened.
Photograph J.A. Walton

The Moor, June 1962.

The steel frame on the left of the picture was to support the new building for a branch of Marks & Spencer, now long since closed. The Williams Deacons bank would make way for a branch of Boots the Chemists. It looks like a Saturday with shoppers out in force. Note the hair styles and clothing of the day.
Photograph C.J. Farrant

The Moor, July 1961

Looking down the Moor towards London Road, there are still tramtracks and a good range of traditional shops. The Morris Minor is just about level with Ellin Street, where you may remember we used to go for chest X-Rays.
Photograph C.J. Farrant

The Moor and Ecclesall Road from London Road, 1964

Looking back up the Moor, some years later, we note an increase in traffic and that many of the shops have closed.
Photograph M. Liversidge

From St Mary's, Bramall Lane, July 1962
Three panoramas from the Church tower.
Photographs J.A. Walton

Part 4
Theatreland

Lyceum Theatre, March 1963

Built in 1879 to the design of W.J.Sprague, the Lyceum was converted into a Bingo hall in 1969, when television had worked its devastating effect on live performances and cinema. It was given a grade 2 listing in 1972 and was subsequently saved, thanks largely to the efforts of the Hallamshire Historic Buildings Society.

Photograph J.A. Walton

Townhead Street June 1970

The Playhouse was hardly an attractive building, but it was much loved by Sheffield theatregoers who enjoyed the best in repertory for years. Many now famous actors trod the boards here, and we were treated to a great diversity of performances.
Photograph J.R. Wrigley

Townhead Street, June 1970

The posters foretell a great future for the theatregoing residents of Sheffield.
Photograph J.R. Wrigley

Playhouse interior, 1966

*Photograph Sheffield Repertory, courtesy Sheffield Libraries,
Archives & Information, Local Studies*

The photograph above shows the auditorium of the Playhouse in
1966. Seating was for a total of 547 in the stalls and balcony.
Many famous names trod the boards here early in their careers.
The Playhouse closed its doors for the last time in June 1971 in
readiness for the opening of the Crucible, thus ensuring the
continuation of professional theatre in the city.

Theatregoers arrive undaunted by a wet evening
to enjoy a live performance at the Playhouse.

*Photograph Sheffield Repertory, courtesy Sheffield Libraries,
Archives and Information, Local Studies*

Crucible building site, 1970

All was not doom and gloom in theatreland. The Lyceum was at least still standing, and the much loved Playhouse was about to be replaced on a new site by a modern theatre with a thrust stage and seating for 1000.

Photograph City Engineers Dept, courtesy Sheffield Libraries, Archives and Information, Local Studies

Crucible Theatre, April 1972

The Crucible standing resplendent at the side of the now dark Lyceum, ready to bring culture back to the City. The theatre was later to become known throughout the land as the home of the World snooker Championships.

Photograph J. Edward Vickers

Empire Theatre, Charles Street, 1959
The Empire opened in 1895 and was well loved for its variety presentations. It was severely damaged in the blitz during a performance and damage to the right turret can be seen in this photograph. Falling audience figures due to the increase of television ownership led to its closure in April 1959.
Photograph Sheffield Libraries, Archives and Information, Local Studies

Demolition of the Empire Theatre, July 1960
A sad end to a lovely theatre.
Photograph W.H. Cole, courtesy Sheffield Libraries, Archives and Information, Local Studies

Interior of the Empire Theatre
The intricacy of the plaster work and the decor of this wonderful theatre can be seen in this photograph of the orchestra pit and auditorium taken from the stage. It was designed by Frank Matcham, the doyen of theatre architects.
Photograph Sheffield Libraries, Archives and Information, Local Studies

Wicker Picture House, 1958

The Wicker Picture House opened in 1920 and had seating for over 1000 patrons. It was damaged in the blitz but subsequently re-opened. Seating capacity was scaled down in the '60s when it was re-named Studio 7. In this reincarnation it became well known as an exhibitor of films of an explicit nature.
Photograph Sheffield Libraries, Archives and Information, Local Studies

Union Street, July 1961

The Sheffield Picture Palace, Union Street, had the unique distinction of being Sheffield's first purpose built cinema, with seating for 1000. It closed and was demolished in 1964 to make way for new developments.
Photograph C.J. Farrant

Hippodrome, Cambridge Street, May 1961

The Hippodrome opened as a variety theatre in 1907. It was converted into a cinema in 1931 and closed its doors for the last time in 1963.

Photograph J.A. Walton

Furnival Gate, April 1975

The Cineplex was an early example of a cinema complex, masterminded by ex-Rank official David Williams. Cineplex 1 and 2 used 16mm equipment, whilst Cineplex 3 was larger and exhibited 35mm films.

Photograph J.R. Wrigley

Odeon, Flat Street, 1964
The Odeon had perhaps the shortest history as a cinema in the city centre, opening in 1956 and closing in 1971.
Photograph Sheffield Libraries, Archives and Information, Local Studies

ABC Angel Street, May 1961.
The ABC seen here on its opening day, 18th May 1961.
Photograph J.A. Walton

Classic Cinema, Fitzalan Square, July 1973

This cinema changed its name several times, having been the Electra and The News Theatre previously. It finally became The Classic Cinema in 1962.

Photograph J.R. Wrigley

Gaumont Cinema, Barker's Pool, July 1962

Formerly known as the Regent, this cinema became the Gaumont in 1946.

Photograph J.A. Walton

Gaumont Cinema, Barker's Pool
The Gaumont was twinned in 1969, and tripled in 1979, and is seen here soon after its final conversion.
Photograph J.R. Wrigley

Cinema House, Barker's Pool, 1961
Opened in 1913, the exterior was clad with glazed white tiles. Originally it had a billiard saloon in the lower hall, and the tea rooms and restaurant were still open well into the '50s. The last performance was in August 1961.
Photograph C.J. Farrant

Cinema House, 24th December 1961
The sad scene on Christmas Eve 1961 when only the screen of the Cinema House remained standing after the demolition of the building.
Photograph C.J. Farrant

Old Central Picture House building, The Moor, July 1960
The Central Picture House opened in 1922, and closed in December 1940 due to enemy action in the blitz. Damage could not have been too severe because it was subsequently used by Atkinsons as a department store. It is seen here in its later days as two retail units.
Photograph J.W. Walton

Central Picture House demolition, May 1961
The Luftwaffe couldn't do it, but the developers and demolition men could in the '60s.
Photograph C. J. Farrant

Part 5
The '70s

Union Street 1972
A brave new world as illustrated by the new skyscraper and the pram pushers in the foreground.
Photograph C.J. Farrant

Haymarket 1972.

John Collier was "the window to watch". Seen here at twilight, the extent of the display indicates a time when formal attire at modest prices was more popular.

Photograph J.R. Wrigley

Dixon Lane 1972

Late afternoon, showing just how busy Dixon Lane could be.

Photograph J.R Wrigley

The last days of the Rag & Tag

Sheaf Market, 1972

A final Look at the Sheaf Market in these evocative photographs of the Rag and Tag from the camera of Jack Wrigley.

Photographs J.R. Wrigley

The last days of the Rag & Tag

Sheaf Market,   1972

More nostalgic views of the Rag & Tag during its last days. The Sheaf Market finally closed in 1973.

Photographs J.R. Wrigley

Park Square, January 1974

Work had started on the new roundabout which would link the city centre to the M1 motorway via the Parkway.

Photograph J.R. Wrigley

Park Square, January 1974

Could we have guessed just how busy this roundabout would become?

Photograph J.R. Wrigley

Haymarket, January 1974
January sales, 1970s style.
Photograph J.R. Wrigley

Haymarket, January 1974
Minimalist Christmas decorations still in place and wintery sunshine brightening the day. In this era, there were no shopping malls to visit.
Photograph J.R. Wrigley

Hole in the Road, April 1970

Sheffielders loved their 'Hole in the Road', officially known as Castle Square Roundabout. It was a feature they were proud of. It had escalators, and a display of Piranha fish and it made crossing the road safe from the ever-increasing volume of traffic. Somewhat ironically, in 1993, it was filled in with rubble from Hyde Park flats to prepare the way for the new Supertram.
Photograph C. J. Farrant

Hole in the Road, 1972

Seen here in its heyday, the Hole in the Road, busy with shoppers at the major pedestrian interchange of one of the most popular shopping areas of the time.
Photograph J.R.Wrigley

Norfolk Row, March 1973

All the traditional premises were still in evidence in this picture, even the Sheffield Photo Co, the owners of which were descendants of Frank and John William Mottershaw who will be remembered for their work in early cine and still photography.
Photograph J.R. Wrigley

Norfolk Street, December 1974

In complete contrast, we see modern trading in a purpose built retail unit.
Photograph J.R. Wrigley

Townhead Street, 1973
The old and the new in Townhead Street. You can judge for yourself which you like best.
Photograph J.R. Wrigley

Townhead Street, 1973
Detail photographs of the new construction and one of the old buildings. The Playhouse Theatre never was a handsome building, being on very awkward terrain, but neither is its replacement.
Photographs J.R. Wrigley

Orchard Street, May 1972

Orchard Street was quite a busy thoroughfare, being the quickest route from Leopold Street to Church Street. Here we see, side by side, Crapper's jewellery repairs and Bortner's high class jewellery.

Photograph J.R. Wrigley

Orchard Street, May 1972

Three treasures of the era, Sunshine Stores for health foods, Sheffield Raincoat Stores for raincoats and the Orchard Cafe for a good cup of tea.

Photograph J.R. Wrigley

Division Street, March 1970

This fine building was erected as the Waterworks offices in 1867. In 1915, the Sheffield Transport Department rented the premises from the Water Committee and it became the administrative offices of the department.
Photograph C.J. Farrant

Corner of Division Street and Carver Street, March 1970

It is easy to see why re-development was considered the best option for some sites. This corner of Division Street and Carver Street would seem strange today with the wooden huts on top of the shops. The huts, did have historical interest since they had been the studio premises of a photographer, no doubt for the maximum use of daylight.
Photograph C. J. Farrant

Leopold Street, 1974

It may look very familiar, but consider what is now gone from the scene: Wilson Peck - closed, Marshall and Snelgrove - closed, Grand Hotel and Buccaneer Bar - demolished, Education Offices - closed, H.L. Brown - demolished and buses - no longer in S.T.D. livery.

Photograph J.R. Wrigley

From the Peace Gardens, May 1972

It's funny how history seems to repeat itself. In this shot we see land cleared for the Town Hall extensions. Just 30 years later, the same area was cleared again to make way for the new Winter Gardens.

Photograph C.J. Farrant

Norfolk Street, 1975
The view along Norfolk Street of the new Town Hall extensions. At least it looks as if the new building will have character.
Photograph C.J. Farrant

Arundel Gate, 1975
From Arundel Gate, the new buildings look quite imposing, but will they stand the test of time, like the Town Hall itself?
Photograph C.J. Farrant

Fargate Underpass, 1976
Underpasses were in vogue in this era, the idea being to separate pedestrians from motor traffic.
Photograph J.R. Wrigley

Fargate Underpass, September 1979
Another view of the Fargate Underpass. Cowan and Barrett had a display cabinet, and there was an entry to Boots the Chemist's basement.
Photograph J.R. Wrigley

Balm Green, 1973

Want to buy a hotel? The Grand Hotel had served us well until it closed in 1971, although many of us never saw its interior. We hadn't realised that tourism might become a major source of income for the city and that more and more hotels would be needed.

Photograph J.R. Wrigley

Leopold Street, 1974

Well no one did want to buy a hotel at that time, so yet another building met the same fate. Note the difference in the appearance of this, the back entrance, and the previous picture of the front.

Photograph Sheffield Libraries, Archives and Information, Local Studies

From Barker's Pool, March 1974
On the corner of Cambridge Street and Division Street we still had the Albert Hotel, and across the road the fine edifice of the old Water Board Offices restored to its former glory after a period of unoccupancy.
Photograph J.R. Wrigley

Division Street, June 1970
Division Street was always the place for specialist shops. Note the shoe shop, tailor, lighting and Lecutiers for invisible mending.
Photograph J.R. Wrigley

Surrey Street, May 1973

Leader House was under threat of being demolished to make way for a new circular shaped Register Office. Fortunately, the Hallamshire Historic Buildings Society objected to the proposal and as a result of a public enquiry, it was saved from destruction.

Photograph J.E. Vickers

Furnival Gate, 1975

In the event, the new Register Office was located further along Arundel Gate. The building was designed to look like, and soon became known as, "The Wedding Cake".

Photograph C.J. Farrant

Barker's Pool, July 1972
By 1972, the Cinema House was long gone, but the Gaumont was still in full use, as was the taxi rank.
Photograph J.R. Wrigley

Barker's Pool, May 1972
A wonderful atmospheric shot from the steps of the Gaumont Cinema.
Photograph J.R.Wrigley

Moorhead from Pinstone Street, May 1972

Not an old building in sight. If anyone had left Sheffield in the '50s and returned in the '70s, they would have had difficulty recognising this scene.

Photograph C.J. Farrant

Charter Square, April 1972

Telephone House was just being built when this photograph was taken, again a typical example of "out with the old and in with the new".

Photograph C.J. Farrant

Charter Square, March 1974

Just two years on and the Telephone Building has been completed but still the work goes on along Charter Row.

Photograph J.R. Wrigley

The Moor, December 1976
Woolworth's thought it was worth while to have a branch on the Moor.
Photograph J.R. Wrigley

The Moor, December 1976
Other national chain stores including B.H.S., Boots, Marks & Spencer and Burton's decided that the Moor was the place to trade.
Photograph J.R. Wrigley

Debenhams, the Moor, December 1976
The shops on the Moor were always busy just before Christmas.
Photograph J.R. Wrigley

Roberts Brothers, the Moor, December 1976
However, not too many customers were buying china this year.
Photograph J.R. Wrigley

The Moor,
December 1976

Phoenix like, the Moor, seen here risen from the ashes is back as a major retail trading area of the city. It even had a branch of Marks and Spencer! However, most of the buildings are rather characterless and make our city look a lot like all the others. Note that buses are much in evidence.
Photograph J.R. Wrigley

Inside Atkinson's
department store,
December 1976

Removal of buses from the Moor had already been decided. Like other petitions before it, this one went unheeded.
Photograph J.R. Wrigley

The Moor, February 1979
Efforts to keep the Moor open for bus operation had failed and it became a pedestrian shopping precinct. Robert's Brothers had become Eyre's furniture store in 1976.
Photograph J.R. Wrigley

Moorfoot, November 1979
Finally, the City centre as we knew it was changed forever. The bottom of the Moor was closed to all through traffic by the construction of the Manpower Services Commission building.
Photograph J.R. Wrigley